Mother, Aunt Susan and Me

Harriot Stanton as a student at Vassar College in 1878.

Mother, Aunt Susan and Me

THE FIRST FIGHT FOR WOMEN'S RIGHTS

WILLIAM JAY JACOBS

Coward, McCann & Geoghegan, Inc.
New York

Photo Credits

The Bettman Archives—page 59
Culver Pictures—pages 10, 21, 29, 34, 41, 46, 55, 56, 57
Collection of Rhoda Jenkins and John Barney—frontispiece, pages 13, 14, 17, 33, 54
Library of Congress—page 11
The New York Historical Society—pages 16, 19, 26, 31, 51
The New York Public Library—page 37
The Rochester Historical Society—page 43
The Seneca Falls Historical Society—pages 14, 19
Vassar College—page 12

Picture editor: Linda Sykes

 Published simultaneously in Canada by Longman Canada Limited, Toronto.

Library of Congress Cataloging in Publication Data

Jacobs, William Jay.
Mother, Aunt Susan and me.

Bibliography: p.
SUMMARY: Sixteen-year-old Harriot Stanton highlights the activities of her mother and her mother's friend Susan B. Anthony in their effort to win equal rights for women.
1. Stanton, Elizabeth Cady, 1815-1902—Juvenile fiction. 2. Anthony, Susan Brownell, 1820-1906—Juvenile fiction. [1. Stanton, Elizabeth Cady, 1815-1902—fiction. 2. Anthony, Susan Brownell, 1920-1906—Fiction. 3. Feminists—Fiction] I. Title.
PZ7.J15256Mo [Fic] 78-25715 ISBN 0-698-20480-8

Printed in the United States of America

With gratitude to the librarians of Yale University

Contents

1

Meet the Stantons

I WAS NAMED AFTER MY AUNTY HAD—Harriet Eaton. But I changed the *e* to *o* in honor of a relative whose name I discovered on an old tombstone. It was a matter of loyalty on my part, and Aunty Had understood.

I have another aunt, too. Her name is Tryphena Cady Bayard, but we call her Aunty By. Every summer my older sister, Margaret, and I would go on the train with one of our aunts or one of my big brothers to Aunty By's house in Johnstown, New York.

Now, in the summer of 1872, I'm sixteen. But I'll always remember those summer trips to Johnstown.

After leaving the Hudson River Railroad Station, on West

Despite her frown here, Harriot had a pleasant, happy childhood.

30th Street in New York City, the train chugged north along the Hudson River. From the window I could see across to New Jersey. At first there were the Palisades—tall cliffs, flat at the top and dropping almost straight down to the river. They reminded me of soldiers, standing at attention in a parade.

After just about two hours, the Catskill Mountains came into view, gracefully rolling and soft with green foliage. Margaret especially liked to see the Catskills from the Tappan Zee, where the river broadens out, or from the bend at Peekskill.

 We finally crossed the Hudson at Albany. At that time

Summer at "Aunty By's" started with the adventure of a train ride.

there was no bridge there, so the train had to be floated on barges across the river in sections.

Then, after another fifty miles, with the Adirondack Mountains in view, we left the train at Fonda, the nearest railroad station to Johnstown, and began the bumpy carriage ride to Aunty By's house.

The house was a square, gray-brick mansion commanding the corner of Main and Market streets, right in the center of Johnstown. From the broad entry hall, Margaret

Since there was no bridge across the Hudson at the time, travelers crossed the river on a ferry boat.

and I used to gaze at the spiral staircase winding up and up under its slender mahogany railing. From June until September we were free to explore the ten large, high-ceilinged rooms filled with colonial furniture. And all around the outside of the house stood stately arching elms for us to climb.

It's not that the other eight months of the year are bad. Just very, very different.

One big difference is having to go to school. I've gone

 to school in Seneca Falls, New York (where I was born in

A game of croquet was one of the pleasures of Harriot's summers in Johnstown, New York. Left to right: Margaret Cady, Tryphera Bayard, Harriet Cady Eaton, Margaret Livingston Stanton. Sitting: Harriot Cady Stanton.

1856), then in New York City, and finally in Tenafly and Englewood, New Jersey. In each of those places they've been private schools. That's because private schools have smaller classes. And my mother and father want me to get personal attention from my teachers. I have heard some of my parents' friends say that it is odd to pay so much money for a girl's education. But my parents think that girls should get as good an education as boys.

Still, my real education comes at home with my family.

Margaret and I are the only girls, but I have five brothers! Four of them are much older: Daniel, Henry, Gerrit, and Theodore. Then come Margaret and me, and finally, Robert, who is three years younger than I am.

Harriot (right) at age 13, with her older sister, Margaret

The Stantons' home in Seneca Falls, New York. It was here that Elizabeth Cady Stanton planned the Seneca Falls Convention, launching the fight for women's rights in America.

Our house is always lively and exciting. I've heard about the time Henry tried to teach eighteen-month-old Gerrit to swim by tying a string of corks under his arms and floating him down the Seneca River. Mother rescued him. Gerrit was blue and cold, but happy.

Another time I was told that my three oldest brothers locked Theodore in the smokehouse. He escaped and, by loud screams, managed to trick the others into following him to the attic, where he imprisoned them. They escaped, in turn, by kicking out the bars of a window and sliding down the lightning rod.

These are the moments that make being at home different from summers at Aunty By's house.

Games and pranks do not bother my father. His name is Henry B. Stanton and, during the day, he works at his law office.

But my mother really needs her quiet times. Even though she has a large family, she doesn't just sit home baking puddings and mending stockings. Her name is Elizabeth Cady Stanton, and I have read in the newspapers that she is known throughout the United States for her fight to get the same rights for women that men already have.

Even when she was married, in 1840, she had strong ideas on women's rights. Usually, in the marriage ceremony, a bride promises to "love and obey" her husband, but Mother had the word "obey" dropped from the service. Later she had her friends write to her as "Elizabeth Cady Stanton," not "Mrs. Henry B. Stanton." That was to show

Henry B. Stanton, Harriot's father

that she was still a separate person, not just a man's wife.

As you might expect, Mother found a very special man to marry. As early as the 1830s Father already was well known for his biting, witty speeches against slavery in the United States. He could make people in his audiences laugh as well as weep, and because he was such a good speaker, those who defended the idea of slavery hated him. Sometimes angry mobs attacked him. But he continued to speak out.

The fight to win equal rights for women also interested Father. Even before he and Mother met he had begun

Elizabeth Cady Stanton with her son, Gerrit, when he was about ten years old.

writing for newspapers and lecturing about equal rights. For their wedding trip Mother and Father sailed to London, where Father was a delegate to the World Anti-Slavery Convention. It's just like the two of them to take a "working honeymoon"!

Father always takes time from his law practice to help

Mother with her work, or to speak in public. He is handsome and charming and very distinguished looking. But I think people like and trust him most because they can easily tell how deeply he believes the things he says.

In 1848, eight years before I was born, Mother and a small group of other ladies announced a women's rights meeting in Seneca Falls, New York. Mother wrote a Declaration of Sentiments which said that the laws should be equal for men and women. When I read her Declaration, it seemed to be a lot like our Declaration of Independence. But when Thomas Jefferson wrote his Declaration in 1776, he said that "all men are created equal."

Mother wrote that "all men AND WOMEN are created equal."

At the time of the Seneca Falls meeting, women had very few rights. And certainly they had little "independence." They were not allowed to vote, to practice law or medicine, to sign wills or contracts without their husbands' permission, or to serve on juries. There were few jobs open to women. Almost no colleges admitted them as students. In the marriage contract, a husband had almost complete control over everything his wife and children did.

After the Seneca Falls meeting, Mother wrote articles for Horace Greeley's newspaper, the *New York Tribune.* Sometmes she wrote for Amelia Bloomer's newspaper, *The Lily,* signing herself as Sun Flower.

 Amelia Bloomer is a friend of Mother's, and she's fun

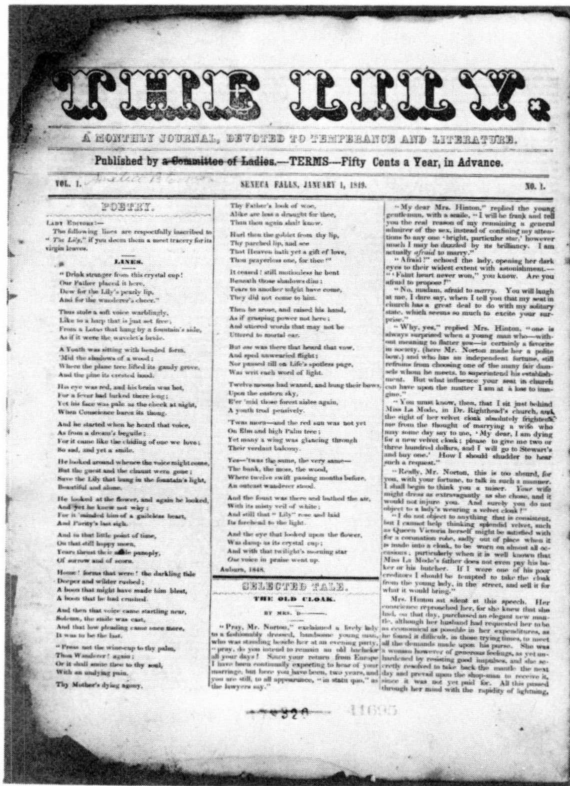

THE LILY.

A MONTHLY JOURNAL, DEVOTED TO TEMPERANCE AND LITERATURE.

Published by ~~a Committee of Ladies.~~—TERMS—Fifty Cents a Year, in Advance.

VOL. 1. SENECA FALLS, JANUARY 1, 1849. NO. 1.

POETRY.

LADY EDITORS:—

The following lines are respectfully inscribed to "*The Lily*," if you deem them a meet tracery for its virgin leaves.

LINES.

"Drink stranger from this crystal cup!
Our Father placed it here,
Dew for the Lily's pearly lip,
And for the wanderer's cheer."

Thus stole a soft voice warblingly,
Like to a harp that is just set free;
From a Lotus that hung by a fountain's side,
As if it were the wavelet's bride.

A Youth was sitting with bended form,
'Mid the shadows of a wood;
Where the plane tree lifted its gaudy grove,
And the pine its crested hood.

His eye was red, and his brain was hot,
For a fever had lurked there long;
Yet his face was pale as the cheek at night,
When Conscience bares its thong.

And he started when he heard that voice,
As from a dream's beguile;
For it came like the chiding of one we love;
So sad, and yet a smile.

He looked around whence the voice might come,
But the guest and the chaunt were gone;
Save the Lily that hung in the fountain's light,
Beautiful and alone.

He looked at the flower, and again he looked,
And yet he knew not why;
For it 'minded him of a guileless heart,
And Purity's last sigh.

And in that little point of time,
On that still happy morn,
Years thrust their [illegible] panoply,
Of sorrow and of scorn.

Home! forms that were! the darkling tide
Deeper and wilder rushed;
A boon that might have made him blest,
A boon that he had crushed.

And then that voice came startling near,
Solemn, the smile was cast,
And that low pleading came once more,
It was to be the last.

"Press not the wine-cup to thy palm,
Thou Wanderer! again;
Or it shall smite thee to thy soul,
With an undying pain.

Thy Mother's dying agony,
Thy Father's look of woe,
Alike are less a draught for thee,
Than thou again shalt know.

Hurl thou the goblet from thy lip,
Thy parched lip, and see
That Heaven hath yet a gift of love,
Thou prayerless one, for thee!"

It ceased! still motionless he bent
Beneath those shadows dim:
Tears to another might have come,
They did not come to him.

Then he arose, and raised his hand,
As if grasping power not here;
And uttered words that may not be
Uttered to mortal ear.

But *one* was there that heard that vow,
And sped unwearied flight;
Nor paused till on Life's spotless page,
Was writ each word of light.

Twelve moons had waned, and hung their bows,
Upon the eastern sky,
E'er 'mid those forest aisles again,
A youth trod pensively.

'Twas morn—and the red sun was not yet
On Elm and high Palm tree;
Yet many a wing was glancing through
Their verdant balcony.

Yes—'twas the same, the very same—
The bank, the moss, the wood,
Where twelve swift passing months before,
An outcast wanderer stood.

And the fount was there and bathed the air,
With its misty veil of white;
And still that "Lily" rose and laid
Its forehead to the light.

And the eye that looked upon the flower,
Was damp as its crystal cup;
And with that twilight's morning star
One voice in praise went up.

Auburn, 1848.

SELECTED TALE.

THE OLD CLOAK.

BY MRS. D———.

"Pray, Mr. Norton," exclaimed a lively lady to a fashionably dressed, handsome young man, who was standing beside her at an evening party, "pray, do you intend to remain an old bachelor all your days! Since your return from Europe I have been continually expecting to hear of your marriage, but here you have been, two years, and you are still, to all appearance, "in statu quo," as the lawyers say."

"My dear Mrs. Hinton," replied the young gentleman, with a smile, "I will be frank and tell you the *real* reason of my remaining a general admirer of the sex, instead of confining my attentions to any one 'bright, particular star,' however much I may be dazzled by its brilliancy. I am actually *afraid* to marry."

"Afraid!" echoed the lady, opening her dark eyes to their widest extent with astonishment.—"'Faint heart never won," you know. Are you afraid to propose?"

"No, madam, afraid to *marry*. You will laugh at me, I dare say, when I tell you that my seat in church has a great deal to do with my solitary state, which seems so much to excite your surprise."

"Why, yes," replied Mrs. Hinton, "one is always surprised when a young man who—without meaning to flatter you—is certainly a favorite in society, (here Mr. Norton made her a polite bow,) and who has an independent fortune, still refrains from choosing one of the many fair damsels whom he meets, to superintend his establishment. But what influence your seat in church can have upon the matter I am at a loss to imagine."

"You must know, then, that I sit just behind Miss La Mode, in Dr. Righthead's church, and the sight of her velvet cloak absolutely frightens me from the thought of marrying a wife who may some day say to me, 'My dear, I am dying for a new velvet cloak; please to give me two or three hundred dollars, and I will go to Stewart's and buy one.' How I should shudder to hear such a request."

"Really, Mr. Norton, this is too absurd, for you, with your fortune, to talk in such a manner. I shall begin to think you a miser. *Your* wife might dress as extravagantly as she chose, and it would not injure you. And surely you do not object to a lady's wearing a velvet cloak!"

"I do not object to anything that is consistent, but I cannot help thinking splendid velvet, such as Queen Victoria herself might be satisfied with for a coronation robe, sadly out of place when it is made into a cloak, to be worn on almost all occasions; particularly when it is well known that Miss La Mode's father does not even pay his baker or his butcher. If I were one of his poor creditors I should be tempted to take the cloak from the young lady, in the street, and sell it for what it would bring."

Mrs. Hinton sat silent at this speech. Her conscience reproached her, for she knew that she had, on that day, purchased an elegant new mantle, although her husband had requested her to be as economical as possible in her expenditures, as he found it difficult, in those trying times, to meet all the demands made upon his purse. She was a woman however of generous feelings, as yet unhardened by resisting good impulses, and she secretly resolved to take back the mantle the next day and prevail upon the shop-man to receive it, since it was not yet paid for. All this passed through her mind with the rapidity of lightning,

The Lily, *edited by Amelia Bloomer*

Amelia Bloomer, wearing the fashion she made popular

to talk with! She thinks that ladies should change the way they dress. Many ladies strap themselves tightly in corsets to make their waists look smaller. One of Mother's cousins, Elizabeth Smith Miller, designed a loose-fitting costume for women, hoping it would be more comfortable to wear. When Amelia first wore the costume in public, she caused a sensation!

You can see from the picture that the outfit has pantaloons—a little like men's pants. Some people just laughed at the idea. Some said it was "unlady-like." There was so much talk about Amelia Bloomer's pantaloons that people began to speak of them as Bloomers. Even Mother wore them for a while.

Many people who are doing exciting things, like Amelia Bloomer, come to visit our house. I have met Frederick Douglass, who once was a slave and now is a great fighter in the struggle for black people's rights. John Greenleaf Whittier, the poet, has also called. And so have many ladies who are working with Mother to get women the right to vote.

But there is no doubt who Mother's closest friend is. It's Susan B. Anthony. Even though she is not related to us, she is almost a part of the family. So we call her Aunt Susan.

It's hard to imagine two people being such close friends who are so different. Mother is round and jolly, with dimples. She laughs a lot and makes friends easily. People say she is a good-looking woman. And I agree.

Aunt Susan is very lean and serious and has sharp facial features. Her hair is short and smooth. She parts it in the center and pulls it tightly back over her ears. Then she ties it in a bun—just the way my Grandmother Cady used to, except that Susan is still young.

One of her eyes doesn't move, and it seems to look out to the side. Since my brothers and I always are into some kind of mischief, we used to be a little afraid of Susan's eye. We thought she could spy on us around corners.

Once she spanked my younger brother Robert. He has never forgiven her for it!

The speeches of Elizabeth Cady Stanton and Susan B. Anthony could be considered "the united product of two brains."

Because of her plain looks and a dull speaking voice, Aunt Susan does not enjoy giving lectures before audiences. But she does it anyway. That's because she has pledged her whole life to just one purpose—getting the vote for women. No matter how she dislikes public speaking, she will talk to any group that invites her.

Night after night she and Mother sit by an old-fashioned

fireplace downstairs. There they plan their speeches and the letters they will write to newspapers.

Mother puts her ideas into writing quickly and easily. Susan finds it hard to write. But she is good with facts and figures. She gives the facts to Mother, who then writes them in language that will excite people. Susan explains it this way. She says Mother "loads the gun" when she writes a speech. Then she, Susan, "pulls the trigger and lets fly the powder and ball."

"Our speeches," Mother says, "may be considered the united product of two brains."

Once, Father handed Mother a stack of newspaper clippings. The clippings were all about Susan's many activities trying to get rights for women. "Well, my dear," said Father, "more notices of Susan. You stir up Susan, and she stirs up the world."

But it isn't always that easy. Mother and Aunt Susan do much more than sit in the parlor and write.

They certainly had an exciting time once on a trip out West, to Kansas.

2

Mother and Aunt Susan Campaign in Kansas

IN APRIL 1861, WHEN I WAS FIVE YEARS old, a great war began in the United States. It was called the Civil War, although there was nothing very civil about it. My parents explained that most of the states in the South decided they no longer wanted to be part of the nation. President Abraham Lincoln said they had no right to withdraw from the Union. He called for volunteers who would fight, if necessary, to keep the United States together as one country.

One reason for the war was slavery. Much of the farm work in the South was done by black men and women captured in Africa and sold as slaves in America, especially to owners of large plantations.

From the time the slaves first began to arrive, in the

seventeenth century, some people were angry about it. They thought it was wrong for one person to own another person. Then, in the mid-nineteenth century, southern planters said they needed more land in the West to grow cotton. As a result of the Mexican War, in 1848 the United States won lots of good farmland. The southerners wanted to bring their slaves onto the new land.

But that made people who opposed slavery even angrier. They said slavery should be ended and the slaves set free. Many of those who were against slavery joined together to start anti-slavery societies.

Mother and Aunt Susan wanted to end slavery. They tried to get Southerners to give up their slaves. But the Southerners refused.

The anti-slavery societies tried to get laws passed in Congress that would end slavery. But the Congress refused.

It was then the Southerners decided to split away from the rest of the country.

And so the war began.

President Lincoln said he was fighting the war to keep the nation together, not to end slavery.

Mother and Susan tried to change his mind. They started a club called the Loyal League. The members of the Loyal League sent thousands of letters to Congressmen. They collected signatures of people who wanted a new law, the Thirteenth Amendment to the Constitution—the basic rules of the United States. The Thirteenth Amendment asked for a change in the Constitution by putting an end to slavery.

All through the war Mother and Susan worked hard to win freedom for the slaves. During those years they spent much more time trying to get rights for blacks than for women.

Finally, the North defeated the South. By the end of 1865, the Thirteenth Amendment was law. Slavery was illegal.

Mother and Susan were sure that men would not forget their hard work (and that of other women) to win freedom for the slaves. The reward would be freedom for women—equal rights with men.

But they were wrong.

Two important new laws were passed after the war ended—the Fourteenth Amendment and the Fifteenth Amendment. Both tried to make sure that black males would have the right to vote. Neither law said anything about women—white or black.

Mother and Susan were furious! They felt cheated. They stormed in anger at men they had trusted—men they had been helping so long to win freedom for the slaves. But as Frederick Douglass said to them, "This is the Negro's hour, not the woman's hour." Women, said Douglass, would have to wait a little longer for the right to vote. First, the former slaves had to be sure of their rights.

But why, asked Mother and Susan, could it not be *both* the Negro's *and* the woman's hour?

Something had to be done. But what?

In 1867 Susan learned that the state of Kansas was going

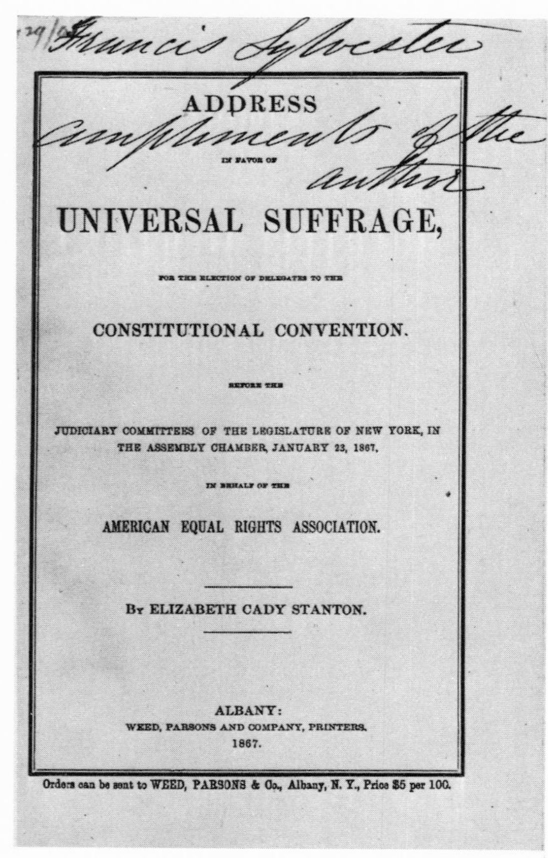

Francis Sylvester

ADDRESS

Compliments of the author

IN FAVOR OF

UNIVERSAL SUFFRAGE,

FOR THE ELECTION OF DELEGATES TO THE

CONSTITUTIONAL CONVENTION.

BEFORE THE

JUDICIARY COMMITTEES OF THE LEGISLATURE OF NEW YORK, IN THE ASSEMBLY CHAMBER, JANUARY 23, 1867,

IN BEHALF OF THE

AMERICAN EQUAL RIGHTS ASSOCIATION.

By ELIZABETH CADY STANTON.

ALBANY:
WEED, PARSONS AND COMPANY, PRINTERS.
1867.

Orders can be sent to WEED, PARSONS & Co., Albany, N. Y., Price $5 per 100.

The cover page of Mrs. Stanton's testimony before the New York State Legislature in 1867

to have an election. The election would let the people decide the questions of voting for blacks and women. Susan and Mother decided to go there to speak up for the rights of women. For weeks beforehand I listened closely as they planned their campaign strategy.

Kansas at that time was a pioneer state. In many places there were no railroads. So after arriving there Susan and

Mother rode about in a carriage drawn by two horses. In the carriage they stored their two suitcases, a pail for watering the horses, a basket of apples, and some crackers.

Riding with them was Charles Robinson, the former Governor of Kansas, who was a firm believer in their cause.

They spoke wherever even a few voters could be brought together—in churches, hotels, barns, even in log cabins.

They spoke in the open air.

Once, Mother spoke in a large mill where the only light was a single candle suspended over her head. She could not see the faces of the people in her audience. But she was told that they had come from miles around to hear her.

Sometimes there were no roads or signposts to guide them. When they had to travel at night, the governor would walk ahead to find the way. Mother would follow him in the carriage, guided by the light of his white shirt.

They ate whatever food people offered them. Usually there was bacon—floating in grease—bitter coffee without milk, and almost never any fresh fruits or vegetables.

Insects, especially bedbugs, were everywhere. One night, to avoid the bedbugs, Mother decided to sleep in the carriage. But soon she was awakened by the grunts of several long-nosed black pigs. The pigs were using the carriage steps to scratch at the fleas that covered their bodies. Mama got very little sleep that night!

Once, in the middle of the night, a mouse ran across Mama's face!

Susan was the efficient one. She took care of the thousand-and-one details necessary for their speeches. She rented the halls, put notices and advertisements in the newspapers, gave interviews to reporters, wrote ahead for ushers and janitors.

Mother had to rest and bathe before meeting an audience. But Susan sometimes spoke without even taking time to eat first.

All along their journey, even in the smallest towns, Mother and Susan found their opponents, the Republicans, waiting for them. During the Civil War, the Republican Party had been in charge of fighting—and defeating—the South. Afterward, they thought the former slaves would be grateful to them. If black men voted for Republicans, the Grand Old Party, as Republicans called themselves, would control Kansas and just about any other state where Negro men voted in large numbers.

But the Republicans, hoping to stay in power, tried to stop all women from voting. If they gave the vote to black women, they would have to give it to white women, too. And it would be harder to predict how white women would vote. "That's politics," Father said.

Besides, many men—Republicans and Democrats—didn't really think that women were smart enough to vote, or deserved the right to vote. They should "know their place"—and that was in the kitchen, stirring the soup.

Mother and Susan needed the votes of Democrats, since

 they certainly weren't going to get many Republican sup-

George Francis Train

porters. But how? Suddenly, almost magically, help came.

A Boston-born Democrat, George Francis Train, arrived in Kansas. He was a very rich merchant who had done business around the world. After he read about their struggle in newspaper accounts, he offered to help pay Mother and Susan's travel expenses and to speak for the rights of women. He promised to work especially hard at getting Democrats out to vote.

Mr. Train had never been in Kansas. Nor had he been on the frontier. At first he was shocked at the rough conditions. But that didn't stop him from appearing for his speeches dressed in full evening costume, complete with white vest and lavender kid gloves.

Cowboys and buffalo hunters came to see him. They wore their ten-gallon hats, their leather shirts, their rugged boots. Women giggled and laughed at Mr. Train's costume.

But he had a marvelous Irish wit. And when he talked seriously, he made sense about women's rights. Many people who came to laugh at him ended by shaking their heads in agreement.

Finally the election votes were in. The count was close, but not close enough. Mother and Susan settled into deep gloom. They had fought hard and still lost.

But George Francis Train wouldn't let them stay discouraged. He offered to go with them and pay for a lecture tour all the way back to the East. The group would stay at the best hotels, eat the finest foods, and he would take care of expenses!

Mother and Susan hesitated. But then Mr. Train made a grand announcement. When they arrived back in New York, said Train, he would pay for a weekly newspaper about women's rights! It would be edited by Mother. Susan would be the business manager.

Its motto, blaring out from the masthead, would be:

Men, their rights and nothing more.
Women, their rights and nothing less.

And the name of the newspaper was to be a shout of defiance. It would be called *The Revolution.*

The Revolution.

PRINCIPLE, NOT POLICY: JUSTICE, NOT FAVORS.

VOL. I.—NO. 1. NEW YORK, WEDNESDAY, JANUARY 8, 1868. $2.00 A YEAR.

Front page of *The Revolution*

"I can give you $100,000 for the paper," said Mr. Train. "But just to give you ladies a start, here is a check for $3,000!"

There was no way Mother and Susan could refuse his offer. The trip back to New York was one glorious adventure. And when they arrived, Mother and Susan started to work at once on *The Revolution*.

3

The Revolution Stirs a Hornet's Nest

I LOVE PARTIES. AND THERE WAS A marvelous party in the office of *The Revolution* on the day the first issue appeared, January 8, 1868. It was less than two weeks before my thirteenth birthday.

But the party wasn't all happy. On that day Mr. Train told Mother and Susan that he had decided to leave for Ireland. He was going to help the Irish in their fight against England.

Even as he talked to them, he plunged his hands into his pants pockets, fishing for money. It was funny to see him turn his pockets inside out. He found about $600 and gave all of it to Susan. Then, after promising to send more money from Ireland, he left.

 Susan turned to Mother and said, "I think that before

long the entire cost of running the paper will be on our shoulders."

She was right. The British captured Mr. Train and sentenced him to life in prison. Although he stayed in jail for only a few months, he never again gave much money to *The Revolution.*

Still, the newspaper continued being printed. And I always looked forward to visiting Mother in the office. It was

Elizabeth Cady Stanton's desk, with Harriot's picture hanging over it

on the third floor of an elegant old building on East 23rd Street in New York City. There was a carpet on the floor of the main entry hall and a round table covered with a pretty cloth. On the walls hung pictures of famous women, such as Lucretia Mott and Mary Wollstonecraft. Off to the side, under an arch, were bookshelves. It was there that I

Although the cause of women's rights was dearest to her, Elizabeth Cady Stanton wrote and spoke on a wide range of social issues.

first read the pamphlets and books about women's rights written by John Stuart Mill, Wendell Phillips, and Mary Wollstonecraft.

Everything in the office was neat, clean, and businesslike. Visitors there often said that I looked just like my mother: plump and jolly, with laughing eyes.

And, always, they rather gasped when they saw Susan: serious, determined, brimming with energy, but—most of all—very firm. One person called her "the invincible Susan." That means she can't be conquered. And I think it's true; Susan will never allow herself to be defeated.

Just after the paper was issued, Susan went to Washington to get people to subscribe. She walked right into the White House to see President Andrew Johnson—the man who became President after an assassin shot President Lincoln.

Outside his private office, she crossed a long corridor. It was lined with friends of the President and men looking for jobs—all of them lounging in chairs, chewing tobacco. Some of them, ignoring the spittoons, were even spitting tobacco juice on the beautiful White House carpets.

Susan brushed right by the appointments secretary and stormed into President Johnson's office. She found him seated behind his desk.

"I don't want any newspapers," shouted Johnson, pounding on the desk. "Can't find time to read the ones I already get."

But the President didn't know Susan B. Anthony the way we knew her.

"You'd better read this one," she insisted. "It will tell you some things about your enemies in Congress."

President Johnson had so many enemies in Congress that by the time of Susan's visit they already had tried to "impeach" him—remove him from office. And nearly two-thirds of the members of the Senate had said "Yes."

Susan later repeated some of the colorful language Mr. Johnson used when she mentioned Congress. It was enough to make even a free-thinking person like Mother blush. But, Susan said, the President finally finished cursing and calmed down. Then he reached into his pocket and said, "Here's your two dollars. Send me the newspaper."

The Revolution started out with 2,000 paid subscribers. With hard work by Mother and Susan, the number climbed to 3,000. But the costs of running the newspaper were very high. The rent for our office was $1,300 a year. That's a lot of money. And we used the very best—and most costly—paper and ink.

Mother and Susan tried hard to get local merchants to advertise their wares in *The Revolution.* But most of them refused. They thought that an advertisement in the paper might hurt their business instead of help it. That's because of the things that Mother and Susan wrote about in *The Revolution.*

First of all, they were for women's rights—and they said so, openly. They also wrote that workers should only have to work eight hours a day, instead of the twelve or fourteen hours they then worked.

As in this cartoon making fun of Elizabeth Cady Stanton, men sometimes heaped scorn on women who tried to become involved in politics.

Susan B. Anthony frequently served as a target for cartoonists, but she came to be revered as "the woman who dared."

Mother said, too, that there should be new laws giving women the right to a divorce if their husbands were drunkards. She said that after most divorces the children should be left in care of the mother, with enough money to support them, as well as to support the former wife.

That got men very angry. They got even angrier when they read what Mother said about the Bible. She said that men used the Bible to keep women unequal. It was the Bible, she argued, that made women think they had to obey their husbands instead of doing what they wanted. Since religion is very important to most people, even Susan thought Mother may have been too daring. Men might begin to wonder if it was really safe to give voting rights to women. Susan believed that voting was the key to power in America. Once women had the vote, their other rights would follow.

Many women who were for female voting rights told Mother and Susan to stop printing *The Revolution.* "You are hurting the fight to get votes for women," they charged.

But nothing could change the minds of two such strong ladies.

The Revolution continued to stir people up. It became harder and harder to get any merchants to advertise in it. Susan borrowed money to keep the paper going. She borrowed so much that soon the paper owed $10,000.

Mother's friends and relatives also helped by giving money. So did Susan's. But there was still not enough.

Finally, Mother and Susan realized that the paper could not survive. A friend of theirs, Laura Curtis Bullard, agreed to take over *The Revolution.* She would change its name and publish it as a paper for housewives. To make everything legal, on May 22, 1870, Mrs. Bullard paid Susan one dollar.

That night Susan arrived in Rochester, New York, her hometown. After paying for her train ticket from New York City, she had little more in her purse than some change and the dollar Mrs. Bullard had given her. In the railroad station a thief stole the dollar!

 The struggle seemed hopeless. But Susan refused to give

up. She immediately organized a lecture tour, taking her around the entire country. Setting out with her usual energy, she spoke to anyone who would listen. Once she even spoke to a group that could not hear her: people at a home for the deaf. Her words had to be repeated in sign language. She also spoke at a home for the insane.

When Susan was paid for a lecture—which was not always—she usually received $75 or $100. She used almost all of that money to pay back the $10,000 that she had borrowed to run *The Revolution.* It took her ten years, but finally she paid back every penny.

Meanwhile, during the Presidential election of 1872, an incredible thing happened to Susan. She was arrested and accused of being a criminal. She was put on trial and almost went to jail!

4

Aunt Susan's Trial

SINCE 1848, THE YEAR OF THE SENECA Falls Convention, men have been saying to women, "No! No! No! You can't vote!" Well, Susan B. Anthony decided to do something direct and simple to change the situation.

She voted.

It all started when Virginia Minor, a friend of Mother's, said to Susan, "After all, you are a citizen, aren't you? If you tried to vote and they let you, they couldn't stop other women. And if they stopped you, just imagine how angry that would make the female population of this country!"

"Not letting you vote," said Mrs. Minor, "would mean you'd be less of a citizen than every newly freed black slave. So would every man's mother, wife, sister, and daughter.

Susan B. Anthony in 1848

Women just wouldn't stand for that. They'd be fighting mad."

So in the Presidential election of 1872, along with fifteen other women, Susan B. Anthony walked into the polling place in Rochester and voted.

Here's part of the letter she wrote to Mother that day:

> Well, I have been and gone and done it, positively voted this morning at 7 o'clock. . . . Not a jeer, not a rude word, not a disrespectful look has met one woman [with me]. . . . I'm so tired! I've been on the go constantly for five days, but to good purpose, so all right.

Then the police stepped in. About two weeks after the

When women first tried to vote the result was explosive. The Police Gazette, *1885.*

election, a deputy United States marshal, blushing and stuttering, appeared at Susan's house. He announced that it was his duty to arrest her. It was against the law for a woman to vote, he said. She had committed a crime.

He asked her to present herself in court.

"Oh, no," she said. "I shall not go there voluntarily. In fact, I would like you to handcuff me and take me there."

The deputy refused to handcuff Susan, but he did take her to court. She was questioned and a date was set for her trial—June 17, 1873.

Even with her trial coming up, Susan continued her lecture tour. One of her new topics was: "Is it a crime for

Henry R. Selden, Susan B. Anthony's attorney

a United States citizen to vote?" That's what the trial was to decide.

On June 17 the courtroom in Rochester was packed. People had come from all over the country. A former President of the United States, Millard Fillmore, was in the audience. Newspapermen crowded the aisles. Susan and the other women who had voted on Election Day were seated behind the prisoners' bar.

Justice Ward Hunt presided as trial judge. Henry B. Selden served as Susan B. Anthony's chief attorney. Mr. Selden said that when Susan voted she thought she had a right to vote. So what she did could not be considered a crime. She was putting her idea to a test. Susan B. Anthony was no criminal. Moreover, women legally *did* have the right to vote, he said, according to the Constitution.

Mr. Selden's speech was clear, logical, and to the point. For more than three hours he spoke eloquently.

But Judge Hunt hardly listened at all. Instead, he read a statement that he had prepared before coming into court—before he had heard the argument for the defense.

Then he ordered the all-male jury to find Susan B. Anthony guilty as charged.

Mr. Selden jumped to his feet. "I object! I object!" he shouted. "No judge has a right in a criminal case to tell a jury what to decide. I demand that the members of the jury be allowed to vote."

But Judge Hunt dismissed the jury without letting one of its members speak.

The next day Susan's lawyers asked for a new trial. Judge Hunt turned down the request. He then ordered Susan to stand for sentencing. "Has the prisoner anything to say why sentence shall not be pronounced?" asked Judge Hunt.

Susan, dressed in black except for a trimming of white lace at her neckline, paused for an instant. Then she spoke firmly and forcefully.

"Yes, Your Honor, I have many things to say: for in your ordered verdict of guilty you have trampled under foot every vital principle of our government. My natural rights, my civil rights, my political rights, my judicial rights are all alike ignored."

Judge Hunt, impatient, interrupted. Pointing at the accused, he declared, "The Court cannot allow the prisoner to go on."

But Susan would not stop. Since the day of her arrest she had been given no chance to defend herself. Judge Hunt had not even allowed her to be a witness for herself at the trial.

"The prisoner must sit down—the Court cannot allow it," bellowed Judge Hunt.

Susan continued: "Had Your Honor submitted my case to the jury, as was clearly your duty, even then I should have had just cause of protest, for not one of those men was my peer; but native or foreign born, white or black, rich or poor, educated or ignorant, sober or drunk, each and every man of them was my political superior. . . . Under such circumstances a commoner in England, tried before a jury of lords, would have far less cause to complain than have I, a woman, tried before a jury of men."

"The Court must insist," Judge Hunt interrupted again. "The prisoner has been tried according to the established forms of the law."

"Yes, Your Honor," answered Susan, "but by forms of law all made by men, interpreted by men, in favor of men, and against women."

"The Court orders the prisoner to sit down. It will not allow another word!" shouted Judge Hunt, banging his gavel for order.

Susan had a final word. She had expected, she said, a fair trial and justice. "But failing to get this justice . . . I

Miss Anthony worked singlemindedly toward one goal—equal rights for women.

ask not leniency at your hands but rather the full rigor of the law."

"The Court must insist . . ." started Judge Hunt. At that point Susan sat down.

"The prisoner will stand up," directed the judge.

Again she rose.

"The sentence of the Court is that you pay a fine of one hundred dollars and the costs of prosecution."

"May it please Your Honor," began Susan. "I will never

pay a dollar of your unjust penalty. All I possess is a debt of ten thousand dollars incurred by publishing my paper—*The Revolution*—the sole object of which was to educate all women to do precisely as I have done, rebel against your man-made, unjust, unconstitutional forms of law, which tax, fine, imprison, and hang women, while denying them the right of representation in the government."

Susan, remaining calm, but with her voice rising in defiance, then concluded: "I will work on with might and main to pay every dollar of that honest debt, but not a penny shall go to this unjust claim. And I shall earnestly and persistently continue to urge all women to the practical recognition of the old Revolutionary maxim, 'Resistance to tyranny is obedience to God.' "

For a moment the courtroom was hushed in silence. Later we heard that even some members of the jury said they had felt like applauding, perhaps even cheering out loud.

Judge Hunt, unruffled, proceeded. Since Susan B. Anthony refused to pay the $100 fine, he could have her sent to jail. But then she would have had the right to appeal her case to the United States Supreme Court. Instead, he said, "Madam, the Court will not order you to stand committed until the fine is paid."

That meant he would not send her to jail.

And, of course, Susan never paid the fine.

My mother often speaks and writes about Susan's trial. She compares it to something else that happened on June

17 nearly a century ago—the Battle of Bunker Hill in the American Revolution. In that battle the American Colonists were forced back, almost wiped out. But they kept on fighting. They lost the battle. But they won the war, and won their freedom from Great Britain.

Mother likes to think that some day—maybe a century from now—people will look back on Susan B. Anthony's trial and remember her as a hero—a hero in the struggle to win equal rights for women.

5

Growing Up in a Free-thinking Family

IT'S NOT SURPRISING, GROWING UP in a family like mine, that I would be interested in women's rights. I can remember, when I was ten years old, making it clear to Father where I stood.

My brothers and I used to climb a big chestnut tree outside our home in Tenafly, New Jersey. One day, seeing us, he called out with concern in his voice, "My daughter, come down, you'll fall."

I answered, "Why don't you ask Bob to come down? He's three years younger and one branch higher."

Mother was proud of me for that.

Our home is always alive with ideas. We debate every issue of the day around the dining table—the rights of women and Negroes, of course, but also matters of war and peace, education, art, literature, history. No topic is forbidden.

And it is not considered right to change one's opinion just to please someone else in the family. We are encouraged by our parents to stand up for our beliefs regardless of what others think.

Sometimes we even challenge Susan. But usually she and Mother carry on their serious planning in private, away from a house full of active children.

I have learned so very much from the visitors to our house. One guest I'll never forget was Sojourner Truth, the famous Negro and women's rights leader. She had been born a slave and, before winning her freedom, was badly mistreated by several masters. One day Mother asked me to read the morning newspapers to Sojourner, who sat leaning back, smoking her pipe.

"Sojourner, can't you read?" I asked.

"Oh no, honey," she answered. "I can't read little things, like letters. I read big things, like men."

For a young girl, growing up in a house where words were so important—especially words in books and newspapers—Sojourner taught me an important lesson about people.

I learned still another lesson from my Grandmother Cady. When her church was electing a new minister, the men of the congregation wanted one candidate; the women preferred another. The men plotted to have the women

Sojourner Truth

vote last; then, just before the votes were counted, they planned to skim off the topmost ballots in the pile (the women's votes) and destroy them. In that way their candidate was sure to win.

Grandmother Cady agreed to the men's request that the women vote last, all the time smiling over a plot of her own.

On the day of the election, each man, in turn, walked

down the aisle of the church and deposited his ballot in a large silver urn. Then each of the women voted. Grandmother Cady waited at the end of the line.

When Grandmother Cady put her ballot into the urn, she swiftly dipped both hands all the way in. She stirred the ballots every which-way, just as she would toss a salad.

The women's votes got counted properly. Grandmother wasn't going to let men get away with something unfair.

Neither would Mother.

Neither would Susan—or for that matter any of the other ladies in the fight for women's rights.

And when I get my chance, neither will I.

Epilogue

HARRIOT STANTON FOLLOWED directly in the footsteps of her illustrious mother. She became a leader in the movement for women's rights.

After graduating from Vassar College with honors in 1878, she helped Elizabeth Cady Stanton and Susan B. Anthony write their *History of Woman Suffrage,* the most important source historians have on women's struggle for voting rights.

In 1882 Harriot Stanton married an English businessman, William Henry Blatch. For twenty years they lived in a small village near London. They had two children, one of whom died in childhood. In 1902 the Blatch family moved to the United States. Harriot once again became

Harriot Stanton (second from front) at Vassar College

active in the women's rights movement. She started a new group, the Equality League of Self-Supporting Women.

Mrs. Blatch and her group injected new life and energy into the movement. She taught American women to em-

Following the lead of British "suffragettes," American "suffragists" turned to parades and demonstrations to attract public attention.

ploy some of the techniques used by suffragettes in England—parades, open-air meetings, testimony before legislatures, campaigning on behalf of friendly political candidates. A Socialist from the days in England, she took bold stands on issues, sometimes causing concern among more cautious women leaders. Yet it was her support that renewed the lagging cause of women's suffrage.

In 1920, when Harriot Stanton Blatch was sixty-four years old, the Nineteenth Amendment to the Constitution became law, officially giving women the right to vote. Even

Under new leadership in the twentieth century, the women's suffrage movement gave up the horse and carriage. In the driver's seat—both of the car and the movement—is Harriot Stanton Blatch.

after that Harriot remained active in public life, especially in the peace movement and the drive for an Equal Rights Amendment to the Constitution—intended to give women complete equality with men. Today, as the twentieth century nears its conclusion, that Amendment still faces strong opposition and has not become law.

The indomitable ladies of the crusade for women's rights (about 1888)

Always an admirer of her mother, she joined with her brother, Theodore, in editing *Elizabeth Cady Stanton, as Revealed in Her Letters, Diary and Reminiscences* (1922). Harriot died in 1940 at the age of eighty-four.

Elizabeth Cady Stanton (1815–1902) and Susan B. Anthony (1820–1906) unquestionably rank as the outstanding figures in the history of women's rights agitation in America.

Mrs. Stanton burst into public attention in 1848 as the organizer of the Seneca Falls Convention and author of the convention's Declaration of Sentiments. For the remainder of the nineteenth century she dominated the fight for women's voting privileges, sharing center stage only with Miss Anthony. Mrs. Stanton's interests ranged more widely. She was concerned with the need for sweeping economic and social changes in American society as a whole—and she supported the Populist (People's) Party in 1896. In 1902, at the age of eighty-six, she died in her sleep.

Susan B. Anthony's trial for voting illegally in the Presidential election of 1872 marked the high point of the women's movement in the nineteenth century. Her speech at the trial, parts of which appear in Chapter 4, is a classic summary of the feminist position.

Interestingly, in Miss Anthony's old age she came to be regarded with less bitterness by the press and her opponents within the movement. She was treated with respect, as a woman of courage and dignity. Her fame spread across national boundaries, eventually even eclipsing that of Mrs. Stanton. Grandmotherly, with snow-white hair and erect bearing, she was acclaimed at women's rights meetings in London (1899) and Berlin (1904) as "Susan B. Anthony of the World." Her total dedication to a single idea—votes for women—is perhaps without parallel in American history. More than anyone else she set the groundwork for passage of the Nineteenth Amendment.

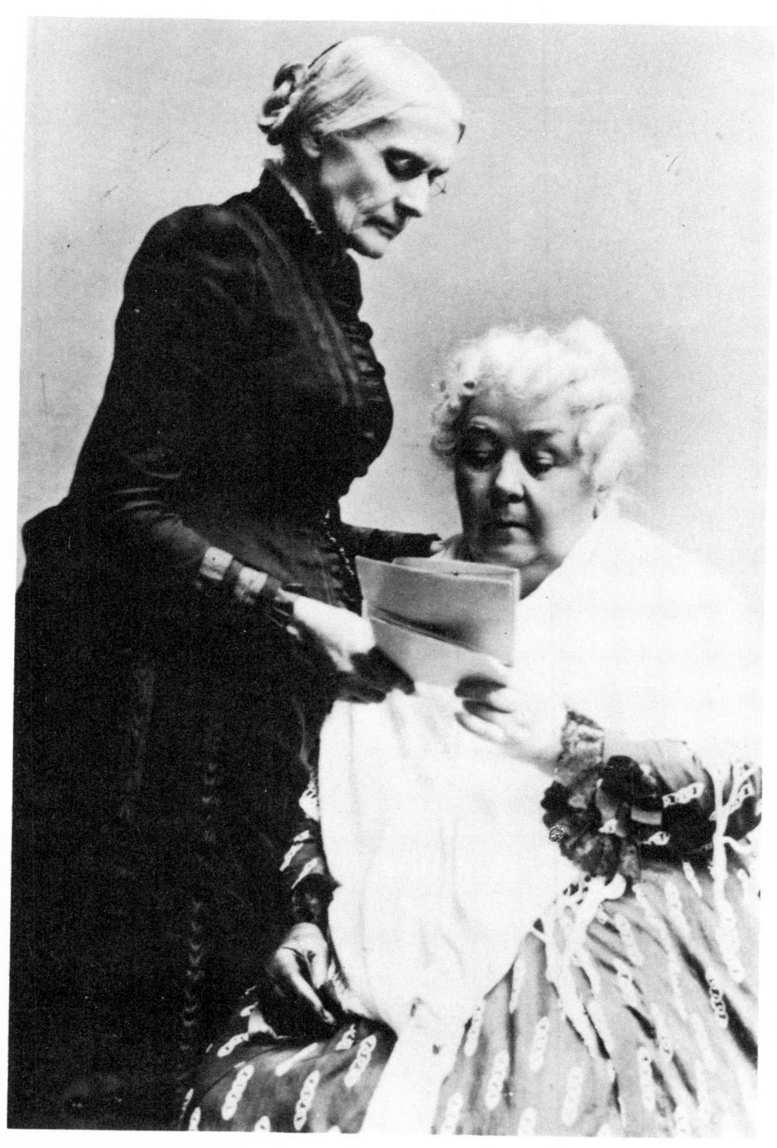

Susan B. Anthony and Elizabeth Cady Stanton in old age: "Failure is impossible!"

In 1906, at the age of eighty-six, she died of a heart attack at her home in Rochester. Less than a month earlier, at a women's rights convention in Baltimore, she had given her last speech. In it, with the indomitable spirit and courage that marked her life, she urged her listeners that in the future of the woman's movement there was only one certainty:

"FAILURE IS IMPOSSIBLE!"

Sources

A basic source of information about Harriot Stanton Blatch is her autobiography, *Challenging Years* (1940), written with Alma Lutz.

For details on the life of Elizabeth Cady Stanton, her *Eighty Years and More* (1898) is exceptionally valuable, as is *Elizabeth Cady Stanton as Revealed in Her Letters, Diary and Reminiscences* (2 vols., 1922). Alma Lutz's *Created Equal: A Biography of Elizabeth Cady Stanton* (1940) is thorough and compassionate.

Susan B. Anthony's life is treated in depth by Ida Husted Harper in *The Life and Work of Susan B. Anthony* (3 vols., 1898–1908). There are also excellent biographies by Rheta Childe Dorr (1928) and Alma Lutz (1954).

In the 1960s and 1970s, an avalanche of books and articles began to appear on topics relating to the problems of women past and present. Only a few of the general works can be mentioned here. For a superb treatment of the drive for voting rights see Eleanor Flexner, *Century of Struggle: The Woman's Rights Movement in the United States* (1959). Less scholarly, but fast-moving and anecdotal, is Emily Taft Douglass, *Remember the Ladies: The Story of Great Women Who Helped Shape America* (1966).

Two especially useful collections of contemporary documents are: Anne Firor Scott, ed., *The American Woman, Who Was She?* (1971) and Wendy Martin, ed., *The American Sisterhood: Writings of the Feminist Movement from Colonial Times to the Present* (1972).

William Jay Jacobs' *Women in American History* (1976) is an historical study which also provides documentary source readings and numerous illustrations of women in American painting, cartoon art, and photography.

WILLIAM JAY JACOBS is the author of sixteen books of history and biography for young readers, including books about Hannibal, Roger Williams, and Edgar Allan Poe.

Dr. Jacobs, who received his doctorate from Columbia University, is a former William Howard Taft Fellow in History and a Ford Foundation Fellow. He has wide teaching experience in public and private secondary schools and also has taught at Rutgers, Hunter, and Harvard.

Mother, Aunt Susan and Me drew inspiration from his earlier work, *Women in American History* (1976), and was written while he was Visiting Fellow in History at Yale in 1977–1978.

Dr. Jacobs is now Coordinator of History and the Social Sciences for the Darien (Connecticut) Public Schools.